coconut

coconut

poems

nisha patel

NeWest Press

Library and Archives Canada Cataloguing in Publication
Title: Coconut : poems / Nisha Patel.
Names: Patel, Nisha, author.
Description: Series statement: Crow said poetry series
Identifiers: Canadiana (print) 2020026365X | Canadiana (ebook) 2020026723X | ISBN 9781774390238 (softcover) | ISBN 9781774390245 (EPUB) | ISBN 9781774390252 (Kindle)
Classification: LCC PS8631.A826 C63 2021 | DDC C811/.6—dc23

Board editor: Jenna Butler
Book design: Natalie Olsen, Kisscut Design
Cover photos: © pashabo /Shutterstock.com
Author photo: © Matthew James Weigel

NeWest Press acknowledges the Canada Council for the Arts, the Alberta Foundation for the Arts, and the Edmonton Arts Council for support of our publishing program. This project is funded in part by the Government of Canada. ⁅ NeWest Press acknowledges that the land on which we operate is Treaty 6 territory and a traditional meeting ground and home for many Indigenous Peoples, including Cree, Saulteaux, Niitsitapi (Blackfoot), Métis, and Nakota Sioux.

#201, 8540 – 109 Street   Edmonton, Alberta   T6G 1E6
780.432.9427
NeWest Press   www.newestpress.com

No bison were harmed in the making of this book.
Printed and bound in Canada   2 3 4 5   23 22 21

contents

coconut

fat girl tweets about pussy

like she has one
like she's sure she's seen it shatter
once a stained glass, once a portrait of a lady
raining down on her like the walls of notre-dame
fat girl thinks her pussy looks better
than anything kanye west could have described
like it is worth more than a scratch on an overhyped record
fat girl has seen it in the mirror and not just the internet
knows its name and what country it comes from
which is to say that it belongs to nothing but the dirt
from the soaked brown earth
from the clenching of stomach and grin
of a good woman, the kind that does not know her place
fat girl tweets about pussy like she does not know her place
like it has an opinion on all the plastic she's shoved into it
like her pussy is yet another ocean

fat girl tweets about pussy like she's raised it herself
taught it to braid its hair and say please
sit quietly at recess,
fight back with multiplication tables and math scores with her fists
tweets about pussy like it once finger painted itself directly onto the floor
into a bloody sunset or a car crash
like its very existence once planted its flag on a white couch
and salted the earth around it

fat girl tweets about pussy
like she used her mother's minimum wage to buy it a seat at the table
fat girl takes up a whole seat at the table
gets stared at by fat men
who have the audacity to ask her to lean back,

to stand up and move, to breathe more shallowly around them
like white is worth more than dark meat
like their metaphors have always been ready to consume her
and still ask her to say thank you
ask her to move all that pussy, to close her legs and walk away
so that their sons can step on the bones she leaves in her wake
and sell the sound of cracking spines to a symphony

fat girl's pussy IS the symphony

fat girl tweets about pussy like she isn't one
and the men question if she even has one
hidden in the origami of her thickness
have to reach beneath her
crook their fingers on her latch
check if she is still breathing or just holding back
how dare she hide that pussy
is that pussy well trained
is that pussy going to behave
is that pussy a man's best friend
kneel, roll over, who's a good girl now

fat girl tweets about pussy because she has to
because sometimes, she reaches beneath her skirt
and comes up empty handed
because if you put her pussy in a box and ask her to walk it home alone
she is not sure if she will end up dead or asking for it
fat girl tweets about pussy like she has a choice
to be licked to the bone, grated to the marrow
sucked and fondled and rubbed raw
of everything that makes her whole
fat girl tweets about pussy because this time she means it

this time, when she says no, you will hear it and listen
this time, you will understand that the universe makes mistakes
and they sound exactly like your name
fat girl tweets about pussy, and none of the men who slide into her dms
walk away with their self-destructive hunger intact
because fat girl and her pussy refuse to be called dessert any longer

fat girl tweets about pussy, and it exceeds the word limit
has too much character, too few flaws, could start a religion
if she wanted it
fat girl tweets about pussy
over and over again
grips it with two hands
plays house between her legs
until coming down feels like coming home
to cathedrals, dripping with elmer's glue and war paint
built to the sound of the first time her mother
ever said her name

I went to india

and all I can remember are the bodies.
        (some moving, some so still)
the sweaty, wintering bodies
the swathed bodies
and every day felt like preparation for a funeral
I never reached, caught in a perspiring traffic jam,
and the lights were bodies set aflame in the night
illuminating the roads made of bodies,
driven into lifelines of palms that were attached to bodies
open for the last tricklings of hope to wash away the grit
caught in the elbows of the bodies climbing higher,
stepping on the heads of bodies beneath them,
        (mangling necks)
reaching for the crown of a tree that looks out onto
an ocean of drowning bodies,
and from these trees of bodies hung more bodies
and these bodies were the tired bodies
the used-up, deflated bodies
        these bodies were the women who stared too long
        at the men who learned too little
        (and too much)
        about their bodies,
these bodies were paid off,
these bodies were told to keep quiet,
these bodies were the wrong faith and the wrong colour,
        (these bodies became breathing caskets
        for the predilections of other bodies)
these bodies were the slum dog keepers,
        (the bones held together into the shapes of bodies
        rib-cage-detained dreams)
bodies gripped in the chokehold of being alive inside a body.

and never have I seen so little reason for faith
so few tears for trampled bodies,
bodies drowned in shallow, seething ponds
where the cats and brown-water frogs wait to be staked by bodies
too lustful for stolen blood
       (and the sky was a body covered in dirt)
       (and the sun was a body that learned to combust
       before the men could set it on fire)
and the water was an unwashed body,
an expanse of inhaling flesh
bruised with coca-cola rings
crackling with the plastic carcass of a discarded body,
and the children on the beach splashed bodies around
until the salt dripped from their bodies,
and no marches were held in their honour.
their bleeding palms touched the earth,
and from the brown grew new bodies
to lie flat under motorcycle skids,
and their bodies were churned into concrete.
their bodies became cities that were once just gatherings of bodies,
       (couplings, fistfuls, masses of bodies)
villagers who once wanted nothing more than to escape their bodies,
and I went to india and did not fall in love,
so I drank bottled water until my body became another body,
       (this one clean and wealthy).
I learned not to pay the begging bodies,
I learned how to close my eyes and breathe without my throat,
I learned how to sink a language in my body, stamp a passport with my name,
       I learned how to escape my body.
       (I learned that I am nothing
       more than a dozen slaughtered bodies)
and I went to india three times, and each time, I came back
and held my body like it was something that no one could ever take.

I tell my mother that I want to be a poet

and do not flinch when 26 years of
licking the dirt off the earthworms
no longer tastes like home

I think we forget that the great pyramids of giza
were burial chambers, never meant to hold
anything close to a beating heart or a living dream
and I wonder why it is that when a child of immigrants
wants to be a poet, we pray instead for a prosperous afterlife

I tell my mother that I want to be a poet
and for a second, we fall in love
leave the men we think we
aren't beautiful enough to abandon
touch palms to the cool tables of our cheeks
hold each other as women do
chest to chest, like we are enough

but if I could write a poem for every time
I have made my mother proud
I would, for once, have nothing to say

chai latte

the girl in the green apron asks what she can get me

before I can wipe the white froth of privilege from my lips
like a rabid stray, I foam out the words chai tea latte

the girl in the green apron asks for a name to stain on
the white casket where she will brew my bloodlines
into something more palatable for seventh-generation tongues

before I can sprinkle my cinnamon-dust syllables into her hands
the spice of an entire ocean settles like caravan into my lungs
my name claws its way up my throat like it was thrown down a well
stepping on the heads of ancestors
who drowned themselves to escape british bullets

I try to show her how hesitation has split my tongue in two
like branches on a silk road
like veins on a tea leaf
like birthright and immigrant's dream

but there is no ground on canadian soil fertile enough
to grow both contradiction and surrender

I wonder which story she will mix into my cup:
that of my father, raised-in-a-fishing-village-now-autobody-labourer
or my mother, city-girl-university-degree-turned-immigrant-fry-cook
I wonder what the chai tea will taste like
now that my taste buds have grown to stand straight-backed
instead of plantation-bent
like a white picket fence

the girl in the green apron wants to know how I take my sugar
how many bodies can you fit into a teaspoon?

which canes touched salted skin before crystallizing for my pleasure?
will the particles stain my mouth red
like the rubies that dotted the rubble of broken farmers' spines?
I know this sip will be sweet enough to almost mask the taste
of guilt and cardamom
that the scent of cloves will travel like my grandfather's last breath
up my nostrils and into the memory of muscles
that never stopped aching

the girl in the green apron expects a tip
I slide her the change I will not spare myself
and hope that the metallic sound of payment
will mask the clanking of chained wrists
echoing through generations
freedom should taste like whipped cream, she says
but she forgets to mention that freedom costs extra

the girl in the green apron slips a cardboard sleeve around my cup
like a noose
the latte sitting between us is full of compromise
I feel my mother's bones in my hands bend around its frail neck,
cradle the warmth of my indulgence and shame

these days, my mother's chai is too strong for me
but I know that even this
will burn my tongue

I do not watch the west wing *anymore*

because I am sick of fetishizing hope,
of cushioning my guilt with the words of white men
who string slow-motion nooses from the lampposts
on 1600 pennsylvania ave like christmas wreaths.

and the only joke I've heard since 1999
is that there are more important things than elections.

and what camera could have captured
the reluctant footfalls of the former dreamers,
the breakthrough melanin,
the children of fight and peril and distance,
the dark-skin shadow-cast memorizing lines and rehearsing them
like *yes, there is survival in these subplots and side characters,*
like *yes, we made it,* even as our tongues are unwritten
to drown out the screaming back home?
which lipstick-feminists will I glorify today?
what well-intentioned bloodless skin
will I blood-let in vain,
which unfaithful sister-victims
of capitalism's toxic lust for equality
will I stand for
in fear that the next back they shoot
will look too much like me?

I fear saviours who never sweat beneath stage makeup,
the ill-inspired acolytes of a charming prime minister's smile
who have never watched their reflection walk out of the mirror
to save itself.

I fear those who have never wished to abandon their bodies,
who spend days stringing themselves like puppets
and hoping that the decoy proves successful.

I fear the faithful,
the die-hard door-knockers who never realize
that we have always had better reasons to make fists.

I fear the permanence of dying,
which even the loquacious cannot counter,
so even my words breathe heavy now.

one day, I will rewatch the finale and reminisce that yes,
I once tasted something like freedom or birdsong
through a tv screen,
that I once walked the capitol
and thought nothing of delusion and year-long christmas lights,
that I once believed that even a fantasy
borne from an addict's daydream
could have inspired change.

self-portrait as tampon

a myth, to think that I am either white or used
one-time necessity to young legs
that carried me across a soccer field
when the boys still pushed back without fear

I am bloodied and burdened
with the weight of growing breasts and swallowed words
taking space in a stomach that clenches inward
I wait for the yank and pull on my hair
wonder which part of me will grow up to be
discarded

two legs

a teen girl dissects a pig's heart
on a bed of stainless steel and scalpel
wonders if it could have remained alive inside a body

a teen girl brings a compact into the bathroom
pulls up plaid skirt and meets held breath
shaking hands, trembles something like
the first lullaby that has ever travelled past her lips
instead of into the cotton-down folds of her childhood memories

a teen girl imagines
that the universe is made of starlight's possibility
to live beyond its own lifetime
and still keep entire species warm throughout theirs

a teen girl fears nothing that her body expels
for she too is a natural exorcist,
purging the last remembrances of leaving men
a two-fingered salute

       everyone who has reached inside her
       has burned the tips of their fingers
       black, crisp, wet and saucy

and who hasn't tasted herself
licked name from her palm's lifeline to heart
and spit up nothing but an answered prayer

rolled a tongue around the dark maroon of stained jaw
as she taught herself the curvature of her own story
how to hold queendom
between her thighs
and have it weigh nothing and everything all at once

and when they ask her why she sings to nine planets instead of eight
she responds that labels are for fishermen
who make a living of gutting on the same wharf
they once dove off

and what is a lovesong if not the opposite of gravity
what is she if not something that is luminous in the night
ice-burning despite the maps she's been scorched from
the solar system has room enough for weak ankles
and gapless columns of flesh that hold up a
seeping stomach that bulges in the name of her own excess

and at 27, when she asks if the black silk garters come in 2x
what she is trying to say is that you cannot call it a pig
if you refuse to touch anything but its heart

an animal needs nothing of hope
to hold her neck like there is nobody
that can take her down easy

I am so eloquent

which is to say that even when my skin betrays me, I
can still fool the hunter into thinking I am some sort of
wildflower, the kind that he will pick for the girl he will
actually marry, and I will stay in my place, grateful that
he spared me, that I get to dream a dream bigger than
my mother's minimum wage, as if she didn't come here
with a university degree stained with my grandfather's
blood, but still: my melanin blends so easily with the
flora, the background benign, so long as I can speak my
way out of trouble and into the beds of white men who
turn the lights off. and sometimes, I open my mouth and
my mother's name uses my tongue to hang itself, so I
swallow down the twitch and the flinch of her body, the
fight that chose to leave homeland and freeze itself in
a country that does not recognize the curve of her, the
twisted muscle that gives movement to her syllables that
still weigh down my tongue, settling in my stomach with
the semen and the plain chicken breast — all the things
that I have been told are good for me — and I have long
since accepted a diet that lessens me in the eyes of my
mother, her name that I cannot help but run away from
for fear that I won't be considered one of the good brown
bodies anymore. as if there is a shade that doesn't have to
stuff itself into the blank white of a ballot box every four
years. as if there aren't politicians thirsty for my ethnicity,
but not my capacity for love, as if this tongue that traces
blood and salt along the necks of white boys who call me
beautiful isn't a double-edged sword, as if I didn't cut out
my mother tongue to make room for white cock, as if the
light in my father's eyes doesn't go out every time I share
a poem that he doesn't understand, as if he didn't leave

his heart somewhere near the body of his mother that burned across an ocean for him to come home, and I get it. I get that it is impressive to master the language that once oppressed you, to march the salt back into the water as if your country was never stolen from you, but there is only so much I can swallow before I sicken, allowing you to feast on the gristle of my heritage every time you say that I am so eloquent.

tightrope

loving myself
is like finding balance on a tightrope:
too easy to hang myself,
trying.

no one believed I was a lesbian, so I cut off all my hair

and who am I to judge
the way you have made your closet commodious,
swollen with imagined lifetimes lived alongside stiffened lingerie
and strangled boys, the thick rust of razor blades staining
the beige suburban rug your mother carpets your curves with,
as if your first-generation thighs could burn themselves acquiescent.

and she asks if the cold was worth it.
so you both learn to swallow the salt — you on your knees,
and her in the spare bedroom with the cordless and a calling card,
letting white lies dribble from her lips.

and who am I to judge
the way you bed the silhouette of the girl on university ave,
finger painting her into your heaving pith
a captured sunset going down between your body's peaks?
what love song will transpire with the sweat,
the damp secrets making a mouldy home in the crowded silence
of the boy's feckless tongue?

and your father does not wonder what's been drowned in the tub
before he buys it, but who am I to judge
those who live without water in their lungs,
the girls in seven minutes of canada goose darkness
splattering the canvas reflexive with every word ungagged,
the impression of the virgin nuns' coifs curling down their necks
to stifle the instinct to breathe beneath the undertow.

and who am I to judge the way you live overflowing
through the valleys carved into the shadows of a closet,
where all the daughters have long hair,
because no one has anything to prove anymore.

age nine

the doctor says, *brain tumor*
and my mother does not answer
I watch my ghost leave her body
from where I am eye-to-eye confined to sterile bed and papery sheets

aging is tenuous in my small body
a carriage of all her favourite memories
that will maybe set sail along a river she herself hasn't crossed
and our song will unbury itself from my body one day
when the desperation of her longing for me
catches up to her like a shopping cart pushed by a child at her heels

and it must be exhausting to face someone you love
and will have loved in the same moment
to get them up for breakfast, put their hair in braids
send them off to school because that's what you know
no one told you of this kind of motherhood
how it is the same and opposite of liberation
how happiness exploits your heart's landing space
builds a home of soft touches and sand
on tiny footprints and dandelions in fists

the doctor says, *you're still a mother*
instead of *you will never learn how to say goodbye*
and I sit and sit on that hospital bed
playing gatekeeper to my mother's future sorrow
and whisper in her ear
mammi, what's wrong?

sex toys

if I had known the pennies would become obsolete
I would have spent them all in one place
bought a sex toy instead of a coffin
learned that enduring the wound had nothing to do
with the gyrating of thick hips on hips
the way she went boneless under my tongue
her body now a pulsating and headless neck
her body all shoulder from the waist down
and even when I felt like my crown was barely there
she still treated me like a queen, still told me that
even living women deserved to be loved
left no room between our mouths for grieving

it was a miracle that we were still alive
that we possessed futures and childhoods somewhere
behind our breasts, the sheer possibility of our fingers
dripping from the mouths of our vulvas like the lovesong
of a sodium bicarbonate volcano

and none of our names become harbingers
or repressed memories
we brought only the fried okra and the biryani
to the party, took home no leftovers
and went to sleep with full bellies and waistlines
that needed no mirrors to draw beautiful circles
of each other

magajmari

how bloodied is the tongue
that razed the hairs on my knuckles
as I tried to pull out the last gasp of a language
     now buried beneath diaphragm
to sit with me on the mandir floor
guide me through this ritual
I know I should pay attention to
but the sanskrit is more likely to belong to me
in black ink on a shoulder blade
than with the gujarati of the old wives' bhajans
as they start up a worship song about devotion that
not even my mother knows the words to

I count the threads of the white bed sheets
spread wrinkled over beige carpet
think about boys
as the children play symbols in excitement

and when they ask me where my father is
I tell them that cricket grounds are holy places
red leather ball in violent coupling with the sleek
upheaval of a planar bat no different from mahabharata warsong
and my father has been in love with mountains
long before he moved to a city in prostration
and when his anger manifests two days later
through the hard wood of a coat hanger
I remind myself that I cannot argue in a language
that doesn't understand me
or pray to a god
that has long gone to sleep
beneath the follicles of my frosted skin

and I am convinced that
krishna was guilty of stealing more than butter
that the magajmari of his youth welded his once-flexible spine
for no one who has lived in more than one body
survives the vivisection of deification
I do not revere a god that has never talked back
to a father with a brown man's baseball bat

and there is only the folly
of a girl that grew taller and smaller in the eyes of her grandparents
the moment she mastered a language that bent another at its feet

and this is how I know that I am right:
to demand a daughter's silence
supersedes all language that I can bury or speak
and when my voice hits the open air
know that I consider all of my words at once
a matter of necessary foolishness

child

I carried the truth
like a child inside my body
that neither of us was strong enough
to name

portrait of myself in my mother's mouth

and how small a cavern it is, to sit beneath my mother's
tongue, swim along her gums, and make a siren-song
out of the saliva's vibration. I once dreamt it an ocean
that could not swallow me, holding me in the swell of
her cheeks as she tried to drip me into the mould of a
delicate woman. I bleed unquietly and I wonder who
taught me the curling scream, the curdling of platelet,
the thickening of aorta to artery—I fill all the space that
I am as a woman but none of the space that my mother
intended when she heaved up my name in place of a
son, and this is the lonesome, this is the stain of living
within the folds of my own thighs, dreaming of joints
that bring more than shame and longing together, I am
the kind of woman my mother once gave a second glance
at the grocery store and perhaps this is how I know to
hold myself at night, hands curved around breast and
stomach, trickling fingers plying into stretch marks, a
body that bends like the universe once did when my
mother asked her to build a duniya that looked nothing
like her own, and in the centre of the bathwater that runs
past my mother's lips, I sing my story like a waterfall
sings its landing, taste the foam and gravity, let the suds
form something like a moon's lullaby to a child that left
her mother's throat, and I wonder if I could have been a
woman made less of spit if I had known how to taste my
mother in my own reflection without wanting to choke.

funeral song

when my father goes to funerals
he brings the dead back with him
lets them linger on skin
until they crawl like lice into the valleys of his laugh-lines
he feels the bite of babies' teeth burrowing into breast
feels the hands of ghost-fingers pry his eyes open
he can't sleep at night fearing that the next funeral
will be his

this is how I know he is a dreamer
except my father dreams that tragedy will one day fall
on shoulders bent from the ravage of raising a family
on ground too frozen to ever be mistaken for foundation
he dreams of daughters desiring palms less rough than his
embrace less rigid, skin less weathered from turning tools in autoshops

he remembers the sounds of footsteps at the door of his garage
the dust that snuck past the white gatekeeper's mask
settling stiff near his heart
the words he held back when he saw them smile
and wonders when loneliness started smelling like spilled gasoline

he doesn't remember trading affection for the house
he built in their name
built with immigrant sweat and bone
but that's all he brought with him
and was ever taught he could be

my father wonders if love plays house with the old cigarettes
down at the bottom of his lungs
and although he knows better

he misses the gasp of nicotine
craves it in late-night worried creases of his forehead
now he's waiting to hold love to lips,
for love to push past at the right moment
he fears missing the moment
just like he missed the last

father, what must it sound like to feel your heart
beat to the sound of my footsteps
as I sneak back in at night
how loud the empty beds around you
that your ears overflow in the silence that stretches between us
what must the minutes you spend alone
taste like when they dilute the words we'll never say out loud?

because when my father goes to funerals
he mourns the loss of daughters to dreams he couldn't fulfill
he doesn't know when pride became safety net
knows he can't go back and hold hands instead of hardware
knows that his smile is too cracked to convey comfort
when the only comfort he can provide
is a future he can't control

there are no more words for the time trickling down his worn-muscled back
reminding him that he is only ever too late

so he lays head to pillow
no tears in sight
holds heart in fist for none to see
and hopes that the next funeral won't be his

autumn leaves

maybe it wasn't really a suicide note. it looked too much like the kind of letter I would write tina on sundays where the sun tried to sleep between the creases on my back with a breathing insistence that next week was surely still coming. the new street we moved to doesn't have a crack down the middle to use as a badminton net anymore, where even the pale drivers slowed down despite the heat and the cool fans waiting to remind them that they'd never left a country too hot to go back to. and it wasn't really a suicide note because I couldn't even recognize my mother's handwriting smothered into the shape of a language that wasn't hers to begin or end with, words that leered deeply, an antithesis of motherhood, where the creases worn into the folds of the hilroy loose-leaf looked too much like the wrinkled bitterness hidden under the everyday red-eye target our women call marriage. and there was no way the sounds that dripped off the page murmured like the hot beating of my blood two days later as I watched my own pulse drown itself in the open air outside my wrists, and no, it wasn't really a suicide note if I put it back where I found it. more like a ghost, pressed autumn leaves between the pages of a book I forgot I borrowed from tina two years ago, thin and dry and faded, reminiscent of a life that it once tried to escape by falling.

the visitor

when I come back home, I tell people how

I was mistaken for my mother
until they heard me say her name
freed like scattered pigeon in the thick baroda air

when they ask me where I'm from

behind a surgical mask
my throat captions reels of rolling mumbai traffic
viscous dust, the three extra hours we waited
after the missed flight to amritsar

how my father swam into his anger
until it drowned the whites of his eyes
how my mother's only relief
was her weak bladder

how I tied my tongue into a noose
offered no comfort beneath the burn of hazy maharashtra sunrise

when I say I cannot go back home

what I mean is that
they can taste a traitor by the hues of haldi'd palms
count the grains of rice I can eat by hand
before I reach back for silver spoon

when they ask me when I'll be back

I say hum lagna nathi karatho

and I think about the grasped bottleneck of wagah-attari
and I think about chai tea and general dyer
recall the scent of opaque topiary soldiers
the way tourist cameras share light waves
with hundred-year-old bullet holes
how jallianwala bagh is such a *money maker*
the bodies that plated the golden gurdwara
and the bodies that lined the well they were thrown into

I think about how I am a tainted offering here:
no job, torn-ligament language, no body desirable

and for once, it is the goriya's touch, my live-in ghost
made sugar-crystal on my skin
despite the sweat and scent of a country that no longer wants me,
that saves me from answering:

never

self-portrait of the artist as acne

and who has lived a seamless life
unblemished by my mother's passing of guilt
I am constantly full to bursting
with tightness and the taste of shame
ready to scar at the barest touch
create a battlefield of romance
I bow down and crouch only for a moment
am brought to light in the mirror
wonder when I'll stop staring at myself
with so much pressure
to change

last call

my mother does not drink
which is to say
she has never learned to drown so often
that even the cork
becomes an anchor

father

the pad of your thumb
was too small a place
for living

how I chose to remember it

the foggy scent of weed in your basement, and the fact
that your ancestors once bleached my great-grandmother's
bones to build an empire, how you used the hard R and
wore locs that hung heavy with the weight of a civil rights
movement you learned nothing about, how you taught me
self preservation was calorie counting, how you couldn't
wear headdresses to music festivals or keep pictures of
your ex in your wallet, how there's no such thing as too
high, no such thing as no, closed eyes instead of dancing
vocal cords, how if it didn't hurt it doesn't matter, there
was no blood and only come on the sheets, I'm glad we
were barely sober because it means there's less for me to
forget or bury inside of me, I'm an expert in parasites, I've
had clear skin since the day you left, and maybe it's unfair
that I chose to remember the way you locked me in the
bedroom and hid me from your father, how your brother
begged me to leave, how you are the reason I know that
suffering doesn't make you holy, that some people let their
scars consume the entire world around them, like a black
hole or a lung infection or gravity, you taught me how to
stomach an eating disorder, crush the ephedrine, choke
down on cock and wipe my mouth dry on a handkerchief,
and some days I still hope you have money enough to
restock the toilet paper or pay for a haircut, I think about
your grandfather's box of useless tv cables and your cousin
maya and wonder if you recall that one christmas when
we smiled across the room and for a second the air was a
mirror or a looking glass and I didn't gag on the scent of
being surrounded by white people on my favourite holiday,
I think I remember the way your eyes looked around a
3am joint, and I tell myself that sometimes people leave for

every reason you can't articulate until they're gone, that maybe god has favourites, but you've never met them, so you settle for sharp goodbyes and thin nostrils, lies and sex, until one day you're incandescent on your back and you realize you're worth more than your ex-boyfriend's flat affect and blue eyes that once looked at your great-grandfather and wondered why the goriya's slaves didn't just free themselves.

if the new york times *still bought love stories*

you never did learn the difference
between story time and dreaming
and when I ask you what you read
you show me the folded-up polaroids you keep in your wallet
laying them out at the bar in front of all your friends
like playing cards, like maybe with a full house I would have appeared
like I was supposed to with your smile in my back pocket
and it, too, was creased like our memories
unfolding and threadbare with late-night overuse
and still you told them that distance is just a matter of time and money
one of which I chased in order to cash in on the other

and I don't remember the rest of the story
because I fell asleep on the phone and woke up in last night's underwear
did you make it home drunk or were you sober?
did you think of me in a way that didn't leave an aftertaste?
did you feel me in your bones as I did you, with a deep sort of throbbing
that kept me anchored to the bed, propped up against the headboard
once more?

do you ever think about the future?
the one where there aren't 2600 kilometres
and a passport between us, the one where saturdays at the park
are soft and damp against my palm in yours
how I wonder if we are happy staying still
when neither of us has ever learned to call anything home
that isn't breathing, mistake a papercut for a lifeline
read between the white blood cells and learn that
you can miss someone so much that you make a ghost out of them

and you must have known as I did
that we could have written a book with all the songs
we wouldn't sing for each other
and if the new york times still bought love stories
you wouldn't have had to sit at a child's bedside
fifteen years past our parting
and tell them that once upon a time
there was a spell that bound you back to this earth
and that you're still trying
to break it

reflection

mother looks through windowpane,
sighs, as her daughter gathers flowers

"this mirror," she says, "is broken"

awake

what is sleep but captured silence. how I wish to be
muzzled gently. there is hot breath held beneath my
eyelid. every night I wish the luxury of waking. I stretch
my body by screws. and who could close their eyes to the
sound of tearing joints. the day's flesh is still imprinted
against my gums. I bleed fully into a feast of wakefulness.
drip vivid down my chin. I hunger for a slumber that
tastes less like roller-coaster rails. I want to relearn how
to lay myself to rest. and who is it that has not wanted
to be embraced by their own body. to be taken fully by
a fleeting void. oh how I wish the dark wasn't trying to
kill me. is it yet another nightmare I try to drink my
skin into. and what kind of songbird tries to sing itself
unconscious. there are black tar sharps dripping into
my lungs off the treble clef's certain steer. I veer off-kilter
rapid thoughts. I breathe the possibility of dreaming
wakefully. how I wish to be quieted finale. how I wish
to swallow myself whole. how I wish to be taken by the
night, greedy for a star much brighter than mine.

self-portrait of the artist as a sari

how to stretch myself so wide
without the risk of breaking

there are parts of me too soft to touch
I fear for the oil and fingerprint
that are lost forever to my folds

I am a memory that lives outside a body

and a promise that even as I compact myself
drape into the shape of a respectable woman
I will return to my unsheathed reckoning
and answer only to the sun
bleached no more

in the alternate universe

I wake up that morning in the same body that still breathes your air,
do not spend four hours in bed,
change my pillowcase three times in one week.
I leave the house,
do not wake up to a headline that channels the colour from your cheeks,
(I will not close my eyes and wish it was me who left in your place)
       in the alternate universe where you are only a phone call away,
       I wake up and I call.

I study all the laws of physics trying to understand
how it is that you in your sunburst body
have made a habit of mimicking the earth.
       I bend towards you like gravity is a choice.
       your smile is the most intimidating light-swirl canyon I
       have ever wanted to lose myself in.

the expansion of the universe was exponential —
building itself slowly, and then all at once
tripping over itself in its haste,
which simply means that the stars were in a rush to create you.

and there exists a school of thought that believes that space-time is flat:
that is, the number of total possible configurations of ourselves is limited,
so eventually, our atoms repeat.
in the alternate universe in which you are still alive,
I imagine that you and I still meet,
but this time, you are flourishing,
living every life that you gave up here,
hating summer under a blue moon,
raising two trillion dogs,
inspiring a girl who looks like me but is taller
how to say her own name like it is a lovesong.

but there are only so many ways our atoms
could have had time.
some scientists claim that this refutes the idea that
infinite versions of you and I meet and fall in love.
for me, this is only proof that I get to see you again.

in the alternate universe that has yet to unfold,
you and I are more than our mistakes.
we become flowers that bloom in the night of our depression.
we are prosperous.
we raise bees and make a million dollars on the honey,
we retire at 35 and build a castle out of stardust,
invite only weary adults to enter,
write poems for each of them,
pin them to their backs as they run around our playground.
we make our love a foundation instead of a cliff,
and neither of us jumps because

you are still alive.

but in this universe, I fall in love with another boy,
strange and gentle,
hands rough from beating on the hide of drums,
instead of sleek against the body of a microphone.
I fall in love with new sounds that know nothing of you,
music that does not speak your name.
this is the closest proof I have
that love must exist in places that I cannot fathom.

in this universe, I learn to love without spilling out of you,
inhaling under the stars that tell me that to have known you even once
was enough.

nine things I want to say to elizabeth gilbert

Author of the Popular Novel-Turned-Movie Eat, Pray, Love, *in Which a White*
Woman Discovers Herself in Asia

nine
your salvation is an expensive plane ticket
          a cheap meal
baptized in bottled water
made by women with backs hardened into iron spines
after years of turning themselves over open flames.

you look like you've never tasted flesh, but I highly doubt it.

eight
when I go back to india, I do not go outside.
I do not go to the beach.
I do not go swimming.

at the bazaar, I cling to the arm of my father.
on the motorcycle, I close my eyes.
I am not amazed at the crowd.
I am lonely instead of solitary,
and I cannot stand the smell.

seven
when my father goes back to india, he litters on the streets like a local.

six
when I go back to india, I salt my tongue
in forgotten gujarati: *I am not getting married.*

nothing in this country tastes like love.

five
when my eldest brother goes back to india,
he meets his bride three weeks before the wedding.
          she speaks english.
her entire life changes in the span of a month
while I lounge on string cots.

I do not know what leaves a worse aftertaste in my mouth.

four
he calls me exotic.
trails his fingers on flesh like I am living tiger-skin rug,
toes sinking into my soft, secure footing.

I do not tell him what it feels like to be hunted,
to be coveted by someone,
to be sometimes beautiful and other times shamed.
I know what it feels like to be shot on a middle-school playground,
to have my hair pulled (*it was an accident*)
to be dirty by birth.

three
when my mother goes back to india,
she points out the dead strays
that have spent their last breath
on dirt roads that no government wants to fix.

she does not wrinkle her nose.

instead, she tells me to watch my step,
lest the blood of an animal,
whose only mistake was being one too many mouths to feed,

soak into designer sneakers that have no place finding home
in a place like this.

two
when I go back to india, I play dress-up.

one
must be nice
to go to a country someone once crossed oceans to pillage,
to visit a place so corrupt that women who look like me,
sold and bartered,
are beaten in their own homes *and also when they leave them*,
while the women who look like you are treated like royalty.

must be nice to go to india and write a book on white paper.

must be nice that you saw a country with over a billion people
and still only thought about yourself.

must be nice to be able to return to a home
where only ex-girlfriends and not heaving boys are allowed
to egg houses.

must be nice to be able to go back to your country.

mother tongue

I'm sure my mother is proud
of the way I whip this language
(that once wrapped itself around her heart)
to bow like lineage,
       (same as it once broke backs)
until it trickles out of bones
like the maharaja's jewels
at my feet

I'm sure my mother is proud
of the way my stories
       (in their white rebirth)
are borne on the borders of my lips,
proud of the way I let life bloom
from the rich, soiled history of my dialect

I can feel her tongue shudder,
twining around the way this land disguises my name

it is hard to believe
that she is not a poet

what is a country

what is a country if not a woman's body. landlocked and drowning at the same time, we reach a border when we touch, and what is a border if not a woman's flesh, the way it is porous, wounds itself and stitches back together, shows the wall it builds. I was told to inhale within a ribcage that expanded within the gap between a man's fist, told to sweat saltwater into swimming pools, cry quietly and alone, for what is loneliness if not the space between a woman's legs, the air that throws itself down a man's throat, what is a man if not a woman's impending startle, impact and ground all at once, where else have we been told to grow if not beneath the pad of a thumb, how do we reach now when we exhale from even our toes, what is a longing if not the tongue of a woman, saying her own name where no one can hear.

on the day priyanka chopra and nick jonas get engaged

my ex-boyfriend throws rocks at my window
until I awaken from my usual nightmare
the one where we are 19 and still together
and somewhere in my memory

I follow him from the train station to his bed
when I sneak back to mine at 5am
I don't forget to lock the door behind me
or let his mother's ghosts in
the ones that whispered across his dining table at 6pm
where the scalloped potatoes sat with red meat that I couldn't touch
and I smiled with straight teeth against his mother's crooked ones
while he claimed white bones all bleached the same anyway

and this time when it's friday at the university and my car gets towed
I do not call him
because we are a province apart and no longer in love
and two weeks later as we get dressed in his living room at 4pm
I tell my mother I will be at the library and don't come home at all

and that sunday my grandmother does not scoff
when I tell her I will never get married
does not tell all my cousins that this is what a liar sounds like
when they intend to run off with a white boy

and in my nightmare I bring him home
and leave home forever in the next
I forsake the yellow-gold and red dress
I think about my children and my choices
        and still my mother does not visit

so on the day priyanka chopra and nick jonas get engaged
and my ex-boyfriend throws rocks at my window
until the glass fractures like the windshield of the '92 corolla

I let nothing in
      not the millwoods sirens
      not the waft of onions in oil
      not the seven-day-late blood

and still, he whispers
what about us?

fat girls rise

the young girls wonder where I got it
all that heft and hustle
pounds that slouch off bones
like melting wax on a candle's spine
their mothers once called me hungry like it was an insult
as if they'd ever have the chance to be full
with mouths as sharp as theirs and tongues
that liquefy in the heat of saying my name
as if I hadn't raised success from the remains
of my own rib cage after the girls
who looked like me had all been fed
and they told me I couldn't just be good
that brown girls and queer girls and scared girls
have to be good enough so that they think twice
before killing you or strangling you with your own cape
and I can feel the men shut their eyes when the mayor
calls my name, hands me a key to the city
that is more dangerous than giving a bag of broken mirrors
to young girls who ask to touch my calves
and I wonder if they can feel the grass stains
or smell the knee socks of the sweating soccer matches
that did little to squeeze the lines of my waist
and in the speaker's chair I sit with sucked breath
ballooning with pride and raw bones
over feet that carry this heavy
to classrooms all the way across town
and back home again

vulva love

the shipwreck sank somewhere between my breasts,
gurgling in the salt water. my body was an iceberg, or an
island. the ship was lost at sea. my body was a warring
country. I spoke to restless gods who splashed their feet
beneath the clouds asking for me to bite. and maybe they
just wanted to know what it is like to drown and still be
remembered for something.

my body is a country that is remembered for something.

my body is a valley of wet teeth closing in on a boy's fingers.

my body is a nation of wasps at war with the bees.

when I cry, my mother reaches in and tries to push me back
inside her body.

27 years later, the stars erupt inside the cave where the girl
palms me. what is the opposite of a blowjob. some days,
I am the restless gods looking down on a warring country,
other days, I am the shipwreck, other days, I am the country.
they all come to me in search of something.

no one asks me where my vulva is, or if she's drowned. *she is
foraging*, I answer, *wait until you see what she brings home.*

dear jason kenney

when only the white men are left,
which deported spirits
will suck the bitumen from the ground
like it was their mother's bone marrow?
what jobs will your people even be qualified for
      when the internet techs and the doctors and the engineers
      when the cleaners and the cooks and the uber drivers
      when the girls at sephora
are all gone?

how many of us will embrace the asphalt,
some at gunpoint, some behind the bleachers of a high school,
lives that will fuse together for survival.
if we build a cathedral out of all the bodies
that will hit the ground in the next four years
and you come and set it on fire, jason,
will your white friends pledge a billion dollars for our resurrection?

jason, I feel sorry for you,
that the only joy you have ever known was in the mortal body
of a white man
that answers only to other white men.
jason, I feel sorry for you,
that no one would have said your name unless you choked it out of them.
jason, I feel sorry for you,
for I have never felt less alone than I do now.

jason, when only the white men are left,
you will realize that your empire was
built on a foundation of my people's broken backs,
and when I say my people,

I mean everyone who is done with mourning quietly
in the shadows of a white politician.
we will pool our blood that once coloured the sky
of the prairie sunset you sacrificed us to,
for we, who have lived closest to the dirt,
know how to taste even this clay
and rise up larger than the ghosts you try to make of us.

jason, home is where the heart is,
and mine, despite your best efforts,
is still beating.

on the day india decriminalizes homosexual acts

I spend four hours at the temple
I rub ganpati bapa's feet
with nariyela pani and fresh milk
my mother rubs coconut oil in my hair before braiding it
the boy rubs his bleach inside of me
nothing mixes, or weeps into one another
        no one cries like I do at a funeral
bapa's feet are gilded in the silver of his effigy
my hands grip the scent of holy water
the girls turn their noses at the stink before recess

the boy has learned to tie one shoelace around my neck
he holds on to the other end throughout childhood, wrenching me back
I gasp for breath, saying my own name

watch all the tongues that fancy themselves cultural contortionists
trying to savour who I am in one mouthful
nothing about me mixes or melts into the other
not my skin on his, not my lamba val, not my convex
he swallows my lack like he's always hungry

I feed no one, I feed nothing

he says no one tastes quite like I do
        I am a faulty cook
we talk about the future like it will remember us

the boys change, but the string around my neck stays the same
I skip rope three times and repeat my name in the bathroom mirror
        nothing takes over my body

I skip school and roleplay the girl down the street
when I climb out of his bedroom window
the one whose father never once called her goriya
        nothing takes, over my body

I fail math class, my mother stops braiding my hair
I wear it sticky like a spider's web
catching the gum beneath the desk
I break three flat irons in a single year
I teach myself to speak like them:
let their words build themselves into fortresses on my tongue
inside each stone wall, I cement my name
and pray that my own erosion frees me
I build castles out of pavement cracks
on a bed of road salt and raw, crystallized sugar
I pull up the drawbridge and close my legs
        my moat is red
but still the boy says that no one sounds like me
when he's bleaching my insides
we both know what it feels like to dampen with a white lie

and neither I nor my mother knows when it happens
that my hands sully themselves in the mud
of a spring playground but come away lighter
        nothing mixes, only disintegrates in my hands
I maintain that bapa's feet were already clean
such is the life of gods who ride mice

some days, I wish to be crushed beneath the weight of something
worth believing in
I imagine my bones as delicate as the spines of panting rodents
I wish to be snapped in half and sucked clean for subsistence

I want to be reborn as a good daughter

I imagine myself in a future that wants to remember me
I sit for four hours
I beg that none of my gods are listening
to the secrets pared into the underside of my skin
or the inside of my womb
that pulsate when the boy does, the secrets that drown in his offering—
I fear I will walk out of this edmonton mandir
with a kumkum chhanlo on my forehead and a target on my back
that speaks itself red on days like this:
where india legalizes love, but still knows how to hate lovers

I take no one home. I do not say her name.
I force myself to pray that no one will ask me why
I'm still not married.

even the punjabi girls wouldn't play with me

walking back from the mac's I pass four sikh boys on
bicycles, relaxed multi-coloured topknots like crowns,
helmet-free, mouths gaping in landed joy, their clean,
undaunted screaming sounding beneath the eyebrow-less
buzz of a 28-year-old nirvana song disguised as modern
rock, and I wonder for a second what it must have been
like to grow up in a millwoods that didn't look like a
snowstorm, to roll up the rim of a cup and see your own
name on first try, to be savoured for longer than friday-
night takeout, these new boys hold a future that 11-year-old
me in my blanched and clear-cut ridgewood streets cannot
imagine, starved as I was on laser n' styled eyebrows,
on gwen stefani hollering bindis back, on parvati patil
dancing in a pink choli at the yule ball, and I wonder if the
sikh boys know that no religion that I have seen will stop
the concrete from licking at their skulls, that no amount
of twisted and braided black mane will outlive them, that
only the honda civics and corollas can see us at night as we
play badminton with broken-wing birdies and road hockey
with left-hand sticks under a street lamp that illuminates
in the night sky like a bloom along the vine of the aurora,
and when I get home, I want to call bylaw, 311 on speed dial,
tell them about the boys, claim that this is how I show envy
disguised as love all at once, tell the streets that when I was
your age, even the punjabi girls wouldn't play with me, but
my mother, with an onion knife, cuts the cord, hangs up for
me, says, *bhade, taste this*, says does it need more mithu,
says no one wears a helmet in the village back home, and
my face sours like the oil beneath my fingernails at lunch
time, and I wonder how anyone born at 3am at the grey
nuns hospital could get homesick, because if you've never

grown up in millwoods, collecting coloured stones like
gravel in your kneecaps, dodging the men who stare from
the benches at town centre, inhaling the scent of books and
summer break all in one lungful, you won't understand
that while my mother didn't raise a snitch, my white
teachers with their somersaulting tongues (bringing up
the white boys with their jokes) all did, and when the sikh
boys cycle past me and no one tells them to cut their hair
in these new neighbourhoods that sound like my lineage
could have dreamed, this same millwoods that once buried
me in a snowbank and reseeded itself come spring on the
bones of the 90s in my body, this place that was once so
unpigmented that even my barefoot steps painted these
streets into a tapestry, I do not tell the sikh boys that their
joy has a price that will never go on clearance.

after all, none of us knows what to say when they tell us to
go back home.

if a body bleeds out on a rainbow crosswalk, does it even make a sound?

queer like	a repurposed tightrope
queer like	knuckles spilling out of an open mouth
queer like	a hunched back against a bedroom door
queer like	*there's only one locked room in the house*
queer like	a too-shallow bathtub
queer like	held breath
queer like	is this how they will find me
queer like	what secrets does a naked body tell anyway
queer like	drawing maps with rusted razor blades
queer like	the skin is the largest organ
queer like	the body is a chart
queer like	the raw hands of a cartographer
queer like	throbbing lines
queer like	quivering paper
queer like	this is a way home
queer like	my body is a way home

queer like a body that is still warm when it hits the ground

queer like	the ambulance sirens that rain down
	from the pinprick stars in the night sky
queer like	the molasses-trickling intake
queer like	take a number
queer like	the final sound of a closing double door
queer like	the doctor that sees the fever but lets you slack into dusk
queer like	you are a danger to others
queer like	if you touch me, it'll catch
queer like	*you are a danger to yourself*
queer like	the danger is not a darkness

queer like	a sob engulfed in pitch black
queer like	a map buried beneath scar tissue
queer like	a chart uncovered in the only locked room in the house
queer like	all adventuring happens naked
queer like	overlapping coordinates, contour lines traced in your teenage blood
queer like	wrung-out wrists left in the twilight's breeze for the parching
queer like	skin that never dries, not even in the summer
queer like	the heart is a compass that points nowhere that you need it to
queer like	the first sweater that leaves your body in a bedroom that isn't yours
queer like	the first sweater that leaves your body in a bedroom that isn't hers
queer like	the first sweater that leaves your body in a bedroom that doesn't lock
queer like	the boys that find you
queer like	the way they see your truth, sinking into the uncharted waters of your map
queer like	skin is the largest organ
queer like	now the body is a naked compass
queer like	*I love you*
queer like	the silence wrapping its fingers around my throat
queer like	my mother's guilt
queer like	my father's anger
queer like	what have you done
queer like	what will people say
queer like	a ghara manthi nikal jao

queer like if the body bleeds out on a rainbow crosswalk
does it even make a sound

queer like   the canary that proclaimed in song when you were eight
too young to run so you
walked
with her hand in yours
head unbent and a mouth not yet barbed-wire-torn

and that's the first time you felt invincible
childhood weightlessness before you fell
back to an earth that never once learned your name
you touched the sun
and still, everything cast a shadow
growing up made it harder to breathe
you made friends with the canary
the children proclaimed your song
this time in adults' wicked speech,
this time in molten rainbows
and you learned then that even canaries die alone
while everyone watches, fingers in their ears —

queer like   the body is a chart
queer like   what a traitorous compass
queer like   this canary heart still points
forward, forward, *forward*—

whale song

there is a creature that can hold its breath for ninety minutes

when I die, I wonder how many lungfuls it will take
before my body knows it is safe to surface again

if I am lost to the ocean,
please leave me with the intentions of my mother
who taught me to embrace heat, chase light,
follow the dissolving scent of dawn
through a mirage of dampened salt
how I tumbled within, letting bubbling pant and huff overtake me
what beast of heart has felt so weightless and heavy that it still
feels need to break up into gravity?

my body needs to exhale to ground itself
I fill the space that holds me, press the capture of oxygen to my
bathing moonlit complexion
I move to the song of the beached sister
how she cried and cried in the fisherman's net
how she parted unwilling and holy forever
how no sun could have parched her of her memories
nor us, of our memories of her

and that is how we speak
with more than the air that passes from our teeth
siren-song whistle in the night
with more than skin wetted by box blade
and if I am bled on a wharf, know this:
you cannot build a sandcastle without water
and it was I that learnt this first — how best to capture
a stream within an esophagus, froth white, and still say
I love you

and if I am to sing to anyone other than the whales
tell my mother that I was free the moment I broke for air

justin trudeau has nothing to wear on diversity day

and no one notices

and the women, they come to the office loud
for once, out of costume
for once, allowed to exist outside the confines of an immigration quota
     — jewelled throats no longer choking on every word
     that once proved their worth
     at a border that looked so much like a drive-thru window
justin thinks, they sound nothing like yoga class,
the kind that the office once offered for free
the same week they hired two engineers
whose names he couldn't pronounce

and he wants to seem adventurous, wants to taste the countries
he can't be paid enough to visit

and those engineers sit around at lunch time
hands washed, buried to the knuckles in silver boxes
passing chai and sachin tendulkar's name on their lips
     they ask justin, does he ever get homesick?
     does he know what he's left behind?
he thinks about christmas and his father and doesn't answer
he leaves and eats crackers at his desk
until they line his throat with sand
justin toes his name in all capitals, praying for a saviour
and when he says it back to himself
it sounds nothing like the apology everyone is making him out to be

no one looks at him

and he goes home, reheats pasta for dinner

and the day after, the women are back in their pencil skirts
pearls around their necks, real diamonds in their ears
pressed sleeves covering the sunken oil-burned flesh
from three minimum-wages ago
they offer hellos in the breakroom
tip their heads to the side, open their mouths
point their teeth at his throat
and say, sal mubarak, such nice weather,
don't you just love the snow?

baby, be the life of the party

the life of the party shows up alone
poured in them skinny jeans, rockin' since oh-five
      rockin' actually since twenty-twelve
the year they learned to cry on campus
begged a boy, not yet a man, for a way home that never unfolded
a paper trail of text messages cut into corneas
at 4am on days when even whyte ave has nothing left to say to her

the life of the party was once a solo cup before a pre-game
stacked identical, red-rimmed for filling
remembers what it was like to feel recyclable
tastes the metamorphosis that is a first breakup
hardens and is reborn a year later as a wine glass
      (walks into a room with a breakable neck)
      (walks into a room and becomes the centre)
      (walks into a room like gravity learned her name)
the same year they stopped hiding behind thighs fit for a throne
which is to say the life of the party has legs like foundation
      cotton-wrapped root and iron-wood base
      cementing her slick to a future where she is spotlight

the life of the party was once a wrist-torn teenager
that dreamt of convertibles and backcountry dirt roads
the life of the party is now two-part dirt road
knows that the country back home wants nothing of her blood
soiled as it is with tequila and ten-dollar moscato
      lives like she is desirable anyway
      lives like she is more than a first-time
the life of the party wants to be enviable
weekend trips and boys to kiss
spends four days drinking

in sunglasses she finds during a montreal winter
      (lonely like her)
      (adopted for a night against a hotel bed-stand)
      (still roadside bound)
and this is the same year they get the breakup bangs
cut at 3am with craft scissors across a rouge-stained porcelain sink
hair like a carpet, hair like a halo, hair like a forest that marks you
  for its own
—the life of the party wakes up as an empty scrapbook
      wakes up as a movie without credits
      wakes up as a girl trying to become a woman on someone
      else's bedsheets

the life of the party is no longer a good girl
the life of the party is no longer a good girl
the life of the party is no longer a good girl

the life of the party wears them twenty-twelve skinny jeans
like they never once rolled their eyes
at the girls in fishnets and black skirts
combat boots to their knees
      —these days, the life of the party is a pair of combat boots to
      the knees

the life of the party swears she will never get married
believes only in the kind of love that lights up the new year's sky
on a rooftop terrace
where no one has anyone to kiss
knows in her bone-china rib cage that love is for girls
who with pink tongues
tell stories with less cocaine and stretch marks

hospital beds and six-month recoveries
stories that take up less kitchen and less lipstick
spend less than forty-two minutes in the bathroom before the party
pinching glitter between forefinger and thumb
hoping it will taste like twenty-five-dollar moscato
instead of the shot of gin taken at the door
of a downtown bachelor apartment to lessen the bar tab
and reanimate her tired marionette spine
the life of the party knows that love is for girls
who have never once looked an emergency-room nurse in the eyes
and asked which lost-gown patient haunts them in their sleep
who have never asked a boy in a parking lot not to leave
who have never cried on campus at 2am
and told no one

the life of the party travels the whole world
comes home with stories in her skin
brushes them now with her palms
against the foreheads of everyone around her
spreading herself onto their canvases
as if their hungry eyes will one day make her feel full
as if their hungry ears will make her sound like a real girl again

the life of the party makes an entrance of her leaving
asks for numbers she'll never call and promises poems she'll never write
tastes names in her gums of all the people she'll never hold close
for fear of being forsaken

the life of the party asks for a hug on the way out
knows that touch is more fleeting than her skin

beneath a pair of japanese skinny jeans
        wears them anyway
ends up beneath cold blankets and wonders if this is what it costs:
to be the girl that everyone loves
        but no one is in love with

the life of the party goes home
alone

when mark connolly asks me why the revolution has to be violent

I think of the hot oil that splashed back
and made a canvas of my mother's skin
how her reflection in the drive-thru looked nothing like the name
on her university degree that shredded itself when crossing the border
and I tell him that that, too, was a violence

I think about a city with coal-mine arteries
driving into tendons and ankles of brutalist concrete
and wonder if the humanities building at the university
that stepped on my neck with its neglect was also not a violence

I think about my father, who drove onto a farmer's field
to play a hockey game on a car radio
and faced a landowner with a pistol
who paused long enough not to shoot
how this was a gift that became my inheritance

I can tell you for a fact
no one who has asked me to write them a poem has been prepared for it

does mark know how deep our footsteps tread
every time we say treaty like we aren't a genocide?
I think about modi slaying muslims in gujarat
and calling it peace and austerity
how kashmir bleeds and bleeds
until the chai runs pink enough to sell at remedy
and this, too, I am taught, is not a violence

did you know we shoot rats at the border
even new york lets them live
which is to say that no experiment in human frailty can stifle our song

you can hate all the poets,
call them pipers, call them sirens, call them dead
we are the subway rats who escaped the poison

I wrote this poem in the wake of a boreal forest
I dreamt of home
the power went out and we wept because we needed a break
and didn't know how to ask for it

and if this is what it means to feel the cracking of the earth
and do something about it
then I give my heart to the planet
let it consume the parts of me that are idle
the stars will not remember my last lovers,
or how they spelt their names on my skin
and held me like they were making a memory
and when the last dolphin in west edmonton mall passed away
we acted like his capture and his dance
were something more than a violence

why is the cbc so afraid to give the truth a megaphone
is their silence not itself a violence

I hope that when the revolution calls my name
I will be surrounded by roses
so that no one can see where I grew the lodged bullets

today I go home, and I learn how to load my words into weapons
today I learn how to make a home out of a war
that has called for the best of me

I know to fire, I know how to fire, I know how to fire
with every word that passes my mouth
my tongue pulls the trigger

when mark connolly asks why the revolution has to be violent
I tell him it is a privilege not to know
that it already is

white queer opens a gofundme

to come back with the crown:

    the white queer breaks out into song
sings it like he once sang the national anthem

(back in the day when the boys couldn't kiss worth shit)

and he knows this like the burn of knees singed by the carpet
of a dressing room
twenty minutes after the show

and the white queer swallows   grows into a man
this one with canadian flags for eyes

says his own name like it owes nothing
sings it like no   brown woman was ever left hanging
               by a noose fashioned from the bolt-ends of
               her wedding sari
sings it like legalization was e n o u g h

    white queer builds three floats at pride

stacked one on top of	stacked one on top of	stacked one
another calls it a party!	another calls it a 'party'	on top of another
invites his friends his	invites his friends	calls it a *party*
father attends his wedding	his father attends his	invites his friends
	wedding	his father attends
		his wedding

    white queer gets a good job

works out to fit into a rainbow crop top
forgets that a heart once beat in the body of
the brown woman in india who sewed it
forgets that that woman still lives

white queer builds a border of white bodies
                              white bodies
                              white bodies
                              white bodies
                              white bodies

   so that nothing like her name
   even has a chance of entering

      white queer kisses in public

            the woman comes to work with a black eye
            this time in the stain of a silhouette of
            the person she once thought she could become

      white queer takes up yoga, orders his chai cold

            the woman wants to taste something more than her
            husband's cock

      white queer is a centrist

            the woman believes that a lovesong
            was once written in her likeness,
            but lost itself in a dehli skyline

white queer sponsors a village

    the woman carries a broken heart
    around like a wedding dowry

white queer adds lights to the float, flashes them to a burning sun

    the woman escapes into streets, this time with a suitcase
    this time with the weight of being forsaken

white queer orders a cake with two men in tuxedos

    the woman gets fired from three jobs

white queer adopts two kids, stamped with a redcross

    the woman starves herself waiting
    for the taste of flesh that melts like her own

white queer runs for office, gets elected
promises that it is simply economics

    the woman finally finds love
    in the mirror of a lost girl

white queer posts about decriminalization of homosexual
acts in india, gets a thousand likes

    the woman gets caught
    with a nationalist's wife

white queer buys a new car

        the woman goes missing until she is not,
        breathing until her body is found
        hung from the branches of an amli tree

white queer opens a gofundme for her funeral

        crown

        crown

        crown

        crown

hangs his crown by the door when he comes home.

        crown

        crown

        crown

what becomes of us

when I bled for you, the stars trickled down my legs,
wrapped themselves around fragile bones
that once snapped like songbird necks

my tongue watched as the hot liquid left my body
and made a home of the scorched grass beneath my heel
dove into the roots of a sapling
that stood in the place we last kissed

and you had once showed me how to embrace the dirt
with a full and curious face
move the muscles of my mouth around
a soft bud, nurture it wet and gentle
and emerge with burrs smeared across my nose

and as I waited at the base of your body, I planted a field of narcissus
sat with open legs and twisted stem between my breasts
breathed a swarm of bees out over this new field of borrowing
for I knew better than to conquer something that gave itself
so willingly to the gaze of the sun

and years later, when you finally came down from the leaves
cocooned in green and dripping with your new wings
I pressed my palms to your cheeks and said
I love you like it was all we'd need to meet the new dawn
together.

questions for google assistant at 4am

okay, google
define life:
define: the capacity for growth
define: functional activity
define: continual change

okay, google
do you know where the last koala lives?
do you know how she is treated like a queen
how she wears the memory of her lost daughters and sons
deep within the follicles of her fur
how even the sound of their laughter
as they fell from the eucalyptus tree
cannot bring them back?

okay, google
do you know what the octopus say when we're asleep?
how they have grip enough for strangling
how they would rise against us if not
for the blood they refuse to spill
how life itself is sacred
even on the ocean floor?

okay, google
will we learn to breathe underwater in time
to save the dolphins?
what of the spiders?
is there anyone who will outgrow loneliness
when we are gone?

[*the scene: a fat woman is drowning.*
there are men at the shore.
the stage is an ocean. no one helps]

and what is the ocean if not a woman
the way men take and take of her body
entanglement nets imprinting on her flesh
the space between her legs yet another man's bycatch
the way they pull her up by her hair
leave her on the wharf for the bleeding
how they hunger with full stomachs for the taste of her
lick the salt from her eyes and say they are still starving
and watch as her coral-reef organs collapse on themselves

I was an ocean once
bare shoulders and whale-song in my ribcage
watched as the rigs drilled holes in my body
they left no part of my trenches unmanned
turned me into a war instead of a homecoming
I should have evaporated sooner
left this ozone and oozed into stars

[*the scene: the stage is an ocean. no one helps*]

and what of the human race
that has learned so little and so much about the earth
how she moved beneath us once
are we not estranged lovers

and the ancestors of this place
those who were tricked into treaty
who lived for thousands of years before us
the story-keepers and secret-tellers that
fought for a truth they've known since the start:

that the universe knew of our greed
knew of our follies and our steam engines

of our clocks and brick houses
of our gold, our borders and our lust

but also of our vast hearts
our clasped hands and protests
our demands and our dreams and our children
people who can still come together against the draining
and the gutting of the ground, the burning of the forests
the scent of coal and gasoline
fueled hope that spills across a prairie sky

it is a characteristic of life itself
that all that is living must die

okay, google
define: life
the capacity for growth, continual change

define: death
the fact of dying. being killed.

define resistance:
refusal to accept. refusal to comply.

some days, I cannot see past the blood on my hands
read names like a eulogy:
the leopards
the gorillas
the elephants
the sea turtles
the rhinos
the tigers, god how I never wished
to outlive the tigers

on those days, I uncurl my back
breathe, drink water like it is a privilege
think of the slumdogs in the streets of india
dying in the heat
it is, indeed, a privilege

I stand at the edge of the precipice
both feet on the ground
look the thirsty children in the eyes
and write

manic

girls like her,
we hang them by their hair
in the centre of the room
and clap twice as they spin,
mistaking their luminescence for living.

girls like her have no time to dance.
looking down on all the hands that rise
to reach her, she starts to burn like a beacon
for all the empty palms seeking warmth in her smile.

and her friends, they keep singing without knowing
that starlight is how girls like her say goodbye, across
a lifetime when it is too late to stop a sun from going out.

anthem

planted a flag between my legs
called it a country

I once climbed headfirst into a war room
that smelled like my uterus on a good day
gripped fingers on wet walls
strung up maps with thumbtacks against the heave of me
crossed marks in blood that would tell my daughter
this is how you build a fortress with only your body

on a good day, my body is
more than a cemetery of carcasses we fought the crows over
you need not sink your shovel six feet in
to find out if I am still breathing

the crows were the first to see the bombs land
and the first to get away
I used the fallen feathers
to grow a forest of curly hair on the inseams
I stitched myself into a walking battle cry

what armies haven't slept in the dirt for just a moment
planted seeds with the split ends of their brushed hair
nurtured them into trees, built nests and marriages
before remembering that they were once marching toward
slaughter

I declare the rolling prairies of my thighs demilitarized
where no man will ever set foot or finger without first
praying to the birds that warned me of his arrival

I stood up straight
they said they could have raised a nation

fed them off the grime on the back of my neck
as it bent forward and snapped up in attention
at the first playing of my anthem

it went something like
they keep coming for my mother
and wondering why it is my name
she says as prayer

and lord,
it's as if, *as if,* they know
I will never be claimed
again

joysong

there is a part of my body that knows only how to ache.
it keeps itself hungry, clenches into a coil for warmth,
shivers under the hottest sun.

and this is how I know where joy is born,
somewhere at the base of my spine and stomach,
untouchable and moist with heaving blood and breath.
my belly knows lovesong before the sound has a chance
to beat off eardrums,

knows how to shake with laughter from tree root to canopy.
I am an entire ecosystem that thrives when I see you.
inhale the taste of tropic bird flight and patient water lily.
you and I flow through each other when our eyes meet,
keeping us above a sky of cloud-cover.
I touch your gentle and slow and respond with quick-footed pant.
we run bare, chase a river upstream and emerge wet
with last meeting's condensation on our lips.

I love you. more than our time will ever allow,
spread as we are between lined palms and unwrinkled flesh.
I hold us as we are: caught in a treble clef's eulogy
for the last time we meet,
bottled in my ache and sore with future sorrow.
I hold us as we could always be: future lovers,
if not for the necessity of a setting sun
that tells me proud
of the beauty of our crossed stars.

my father's feet land here in the 80s and

they ask how he's adjusting to the snow,
as if he hadn't gone numb seconds from leaving his mother's embrace,
his body writes the lyrics to a future homecoming song.
melting promises in the prairie frost,
he breaks covenant with every step he takes.
and no part of him is made for this type of goodbye.
the forever, lifetime-across-the-ocean kind
that leaves more behind on the dandi beach than he takes with him,
and now he understands why he arrives with nothing.

he knows that the next time they meet,
she will be sleeping wrapped in only the white cloth
that will never be stained.
that he will cross years to be too late to say hello again.

they ask how he's adjusting to the snow.
it's not the cold that numbs him,
but the way the grey bleaches the song from his skin,
     and he remembers that his heart is stained with forever-goodbyes
     that his heart can't be crushed under broken awnings
     that his heart feeds frozen pipes without bursting
—and it's not the ice that numbs him,
but the way the frozen water perforates his lungs
and how he was never quite told
he would one day long for samapur's unforgiving sun
that knows only how to love so deeply
it burns.

and when he catches the way his mother's voice freezes
from across a lifetime,
the frost bites back words like
I miss you and *I'm sorry I couldn't stay.*

and he tries to chip the icy wrap of that old homecoming song.
tries to remember why he gave her a forever-goodbye,
tries to remember that years from now, he will look into my eyes
and find the answer,
and it's not the snow that chills him,
but the way his heart's been kindling
since the day he left.

he fears that parts of him
are too damp now,
that he will never thaw enough to find his conclusion in ashes.
branded beneath the smoulder of white,
he surrenders his own homecoming song,
knows that the only way he will see her again
is through the brightest flames
of a funeral pyre.

they ask how he's adjusting to the snow.
as if he hasn't spent 30 years being run over by the spokes of snowflakes.
with chapped lips, he sings that old homecoming like lullaby.

I am my father's happy ending,
but a part of me will never stop feeling
like his forever-goodbye.

grief

sometimes I wake without your name beside me, empty
bed, bereft silhouette of a person once warm in the night,
now a ghost-fleeting, now a spirit-shadow, with a weight
that once bent this mattress heavy / I used to curve
toward you, I used to wear your smile to sleep, I used
to curl upon myself and wait for you to take me to the
sky / and I admit that nowadays, I fall into your absence
like there is nowhere else I'd rather be but following you
/ and only the sound of your leaving weighs me down,
anchors me like thick rust, I scrape my wrists and poison
my blood on your residue, take refuge in a body that has
now become a walking mausoleum / I spent weeks on my
knees at your altar / I carried your flowers in a pulsating
heart that beats to your last footsteps / I twisted my bones
into the shape of your rib cage, broke them and set them
into a portrait I could touch once more / I walked your
halls, placed my palm against your candied glass, begged
for you to let me in, fogged the mirror with my breath as
I carved your love song into a future we both could have
wanted / I say a name that isn't yours and still taste the
way the stars tell me you are safe / you are the opposite
of obscurity, you are living proof of heartbreak, you are
deafening love / I sing your story and the children weep
for not knowing you / I tell them that you are here, I tell
them that you are joy, I tell them that benevolence learned
your name and climbed a mountain, I tell them that you
touched the sun, showed it how to brush the earth with
a lover's caress / mon amour, how this world was made
better for knowing you, how I ensnare you now, hold you
close to a chest once emptied just for you, how you fill me
still with every known name for patience, for surely we

will meet again in a lifetime weaned on roses / surely we who met once have already bent the universe to our will / surely we who bed memory and wake to moonlight, we who travel wet and wounded but reach together just the same / will share the twilight's sleep once more / what a life it is without you / what a life I have still to live / what a life we had once and forever / what a life, to have seen you smile at the stars, having taught them how to shine.

conversation(s) from the artist to her mother

in gujarati, I do not know how to say I am enough

je suis assez
—how I too wish I could have suspended myself indefinite
a goldfish-girl forever, scales and skin iridescent,
exhaling myself into the bowl that would hold
enough float to breathe in the artificial sunrise,
the yellow garama
the warmth of meeting your expectations
with the hope that I would one day build a sandcastle-dream
that looked so much like the nine-to-five of yours

(a desk, a plant, a paycheck)

the lifeblood of your forfeited years
that you mixed and cemented to build this house around us
would be the only part of me that stayed an anchor
so long as my tanked ambition fit into glass walls
for the rest of the world to tap at, to cherish

instead I learn to suck on sour guilt,
(j'ai un rêve, kkum, mane sarama lage che)
for still I dream, and I am ashamed.

in gujarati, I do not know how to say I love you.
instead, I learn it in french class
study the way it fits unspoken between my teeth
(je t'aime)

I still have yet to find it a landed home,
a shelf on my wall to infuse it with the spices' scents
(garam masala, jiru, hing) that permeate

in this house, we do not know how to say I love you
without an acerbic aftertaste,
I wonder how I can love the coat hangers,
the velan, the rolling pins that leave no marks
I do not pass french class,
but at home, I master the body language
of anger, of dishonour
j'ai peur, j'ai peur, j'ai peur
that only a child's skin can pen

in gujarati, avec toi, je ne parle pas d'amour
(with you, I do not speak of love)
if I do, my lips bend unwilling and fragile, brittle with the cold,
tongue scraping the fragments of a dialect you call home
like chipped ice to melt in your mouth,
something that once resembled a conversation
you'd fancied having with me,
a daughter you wished had built herself into dreams
worth leaving a life behind for
(pourquoi es-tu une artiste)
in gujarati, je ne suis pas comme tois,
I am nothing like you
dis-moi, ça valait le coup?
(was it worth it?)

in gujarati, je suis seule
I try to wash your mother's eyes across the sink
with the stained-black-ink water,
with yesterday's paintbrush-runoff dreams
and follow as the colour once more crowds
down the mouth of a drain that has seen too much of me

not to taste all the salted ways that I have tried to love myself
into being une fille parfait (areumdaun, sari chokari)
and in the rest of my empty verses
and blank canvasses
(je suis une artiste)
I write je suis désolé, mianhae, mane mapha karo
I am sorry, I am sorry, I am sorry

Acknowledgements

I want to thank the Edmonton Arts Council for their
generous support of the writing of the first manuscript
that became this book. In 2018, I pursued art full-time and
did so with the investment from community that built
the foundation for my career. Versions of some of these
poems have appeared in my chapbooks, *Limited Success,*
Water, and *I See You.* Some of these poems have also
appeared in *The Polyglot, Prometheus Dreaming, High*
Shelf Press, and *The Closed Eye Open.* Many of these poems,
however, had their first homes in dirty venues and café
bars and grand stages and festival competitions hundreds
of times over. I owe the stage almost every good part of
my life: my career, my practice, my love, my dreams.

My sincere thanks go out to some of my earliest mentors,
Matthew Stepanic, the one and only Megan Dart, always
Timiro Mohamed, and forever-a-poet, Katherine Abbass.
And especially my one true love, my best, my red string,
Matthew James Weigel, who teaches me about compassion
and patience with myself and with this land, Treaty 6, on
which we build our life together.

I wanted to write the book I should have read, so I tried,
and some days I think that maybe I did. One day, when my
words are forgotten, I hope the people I reached live on.

Thank you to everyone who have (online and IRL), in
small and big ways, supported this life and this journey.
It is a hard one, but a good one.

In 2017, to honour NeWest Press' 40th anniversary, we inaugurated a new poetry series to go alongside our Nunatak First Fiction, Prairie Play, and Writer as Critic series: Crow Said Poetry. Crow Said is named in honour of Robert Kroetsch's foundational 1977 novel *What The Crow Said*. The series aims to shed light on places and people outside of the literary mainstream. It is our intention that the poets featured in this series will continue Robert Kroetsch's literary tradition of innovation, interrogation, and generosity of spirit.

Nisha Patel is a queer spoken word poet and artist. She is the City of Edmonton's 8th Poet Laureate and the 2019 Canadian Individual Slam Champion. She is a prominent organizer and community builder, having worked with festivals across Canada, participating in both the Canadian Festival of Spoken Word and the Canadian Individual Slam Championship. Her chapbooks, *Limited Success, Water,* and *I See You* have reached audiences around the world with their discussions of family and grief, racism, and feminism. Over the years, Nisha has led many workshops and performed from small town Moose Jaw to metropolitan Seoul, South Korea over the course of four national and international tours. With nearly 200 performances to date, Nisha is committed to furthering her goals of reaching audiences that need it and the pursuit of excellence in spoken word. To that end, she has self-started community-focused residencies and mentored poets from multiple disciplines, curated showcases, taught performance and writing, and worked within new genres. In 2019, she co-founded a national queer femme South Asian artist collective, Maza Arts, and co-founded Moon Jelly House, a publishing house centring the work of marginalized poets.